Rhymes of Our Times

John Cotter

The Avenue Publishing

©A.J.R. Cotter 2022. All rights reserved.
Enquiries to TheAvenuePublishing@gmail.com

First published: February 2022

Cover photo: Approach to Victoria Night Market, Melbourne 2020

Contents

Gentle Reader	vi
The Sun	1
The Shy Suitor	2
Soil	3
Carlton Marshes, Suffolk, England	4
Fifty	5
Australian Eucalypts	7
Plants	8
Animals	9
ANZAC rains	10
Fungus	11
The Indecisivist	12
Ginger Michaela	13
Bright Gleams the Dream	16
Land	17
Sharks	18
Men!	19
Death	20
A Macho Manager	21
Inspiration	23
Water is Everywhere – 7 Sketches	24
The Oceans	26
Air	27
Life Could be Verse	28
Underneath	30
Vandalism in the Cemetery	31
The Sea	32

A Parliamentary politician	33
Wind	36
Separation	38
My Faithless Religion	40
Freedom	43
Index of first lines	44

Preface

As the 21st century matures, our lives must surely be changing faster than ever before because of, for example, new technology, global communications, changing social norms, and exploitation of almost every part of planet Earth. The following rhymes on varied subjects result from happily living and thinking through this period both in Suffolk, England and, later in life, in central Victoria, Australia. I enjoyed writing them. Maybe someone will enjoy reading them.

I now live in retirement after forty years as an environmental scientist working in the UK, Europe and Australia. My interests include nature, science, families, getting about on a bike or in boots, and making things. My favourite poets include Walter Garstang (encountered while studying marine zoology), C J Dennis (thanks Al Holmes, John Dereham, Rosemary Morgan), Banjo Patterson, and Robert Service (thanks Jon McGill). Barbara Birt told me thoughts that prompted 'Freedom' and, along with Al Holmes provided helpful comments on a draft. Stephen Fry's 'The Ode Less Travelled' guided me pleasurably through poetic rhyming, metre and forms, a subject that, I remember, I hated at school. I found rhymes and synonyms on rhymezone.com, information on Wikipedia, and words in Collins' admirably clear (UK English) Dictionary and Thesaurus. Ian Fosten got me started with reading my poetic attempts in public at the Seagull Theatre, Lowestoft. Last but not least, I am grateful daily to my kind parents, Isabel and Ken, for foregoing much to give me a thorough education, and to Fadia, my wife, who has tirelessly supported me and is always my first sounding board.

John Cotter
Victoria, Australia
December 2021

Gentle Reader . . .

G entle reader, perhaps you've some time for a rhyme,
Sitting down in your chair, feeling loose and relaxed?
Why not linger right there for some rhymes of our time?
Have no fear that your brain will be dreadfully taxed.
Motley verses are ordered without any plan –
It's my adage for life to mix whimsy with grit.
So, on one page, there's nonsense of which I'm a fan,
On the next, crusty thoughts from old age I submit.

In this text, I present silly stuff and satire.
Alongside, I acknowledge meek Nature's broad drifts
That sustain and enrich, though our minds scarce enquire
What these are, or the worth to us all of those gifts.
I write also of war to remember the bold.
Likewise, illness and God prompt poems to type.
I have learned that the simplest of ways are the gold
We should find while we're young to enjoy when we're ripe.

Please turn over . . .

The Sun

Your day's work starts with glowing, velvet hold
  On Earth's most eastern shadow, warning Night's
Companion, furtive dew, that ling'ring cold
Will soon be banished 'neath your regal heights.
Chameleon-like, you change your rising disc
From orange fire to rapier white. No eye
May glimpse your God-like state for blindness' risk;
All life beholds your azure palace, Sky.

Oh! Had you not divorced your partner, Rain,
And danced away with swirling Champagne Leaves!
A feast of green would mantle northern plain;
A host of beasts would praise where dust now grieves.
Thank heav'n you tire from each day's work, and rest,
Releasing dreams and stars at Night's behest.

The Shy Suitor

A BOLD man who's intent on romance
Will invite his girl out for a dance
>But,
>>I know in advance
>>That my stance is askance
>>At the chance of a dance.

Gentlemen may not pause for one blink
When they ask to join her for a drink
>But,
>>What thoughts will she think
>>When I shrink at the brink
>>From the clink of a drink?

Very fine as a gift is perfume
That would make her turn heads in a room
>But,
>>I can't just presume
>>That *our* zoom would resume
>>When her bloom casts a plume.

What about a brand new party dress
With finesse that will surely impress?
>But,
>>I'll surely obsess
>>Under stress and confess
>>My excess of largesse.

I could visit our town flower shop
The one next to the local Co-op
>But,
>>Their stored floral crop
>>Mostly flops from the top
>>Unless stopped with a prop.

I thought too of a sparkling new jewel
Such as fuels connubial dual
    But,
        The cost would be cruel
        For renewal each Yule
        Of her jewel accrual.

That just leaves a good countryside walk
A chance for us to talk . . .
    She likes a good natter.

Soil

Endless, clasping mesh of whispy, fungal
Hyphae suck their humic food round tussling
Roots absorbing salts in pitch-black jungle
Populated by microbes a-bustling,
Multi-legged bugs, earthworms slow pulsing
Through their slimy tubes and hard or sodden
Mud-lined caves where roundworms swarm, convulsing.
Darkness lives despite being ploughed or trodden.

Soil, the tireless serf of our subsistence,
Serving plants as womb and stubborn holdfast,
Undemanding host of stocks' agistments,
Ground from elements of Earth's untold past.
We must tame the cut of wind and waters,
Must bequeath it richer to our daughters.

Carlton Marshes, Suffolk, England

I LOVE the leaves
That spring-time fabrics weave
   That change far-stretching land
   To textured band
      Sometimes velvet soft
      Green baize for wooded loft
         Sometimes coarse, unravelled tweeds
         Frayed by thorns and sharp-edged reeds.

I love the leaves
That rustle in the breeze
   That turn bright summer light
   To softer sight
      Sometimes yellow-green
      Stars sparkling in between
         Sometimes dark, unreflecting,
         Sharp blue skies re-directing.

I love the leaves
That tumble from the trees
   That feel chilled, frosty pains
   As autumn's gains
      Sometimes tinting views
      With gilded, earthy hues
         Sometimes source of muffled sounds –
         Kids at play in wind-blown mounds.

I love the leaves
That suffer winter's freeze
   That are forever green
   Through biting scene
      Sometimes dark and dour
      Biding springtime's power
         Sometimes white, powder-dusted,
         Sunshine-struck, jewel-encrusted.

Fifty

Dear vultures all, you've gathered here
To gloat upon my fiftieth year.
Yet,
    Save death, you too will meet this fate,
    Unless, of course, you're now post-date.
    So, since I'm here before the mike
    I may's well tell what fifty's like.

My back and bones are at the stage
Of 'S' for 'stoop' in lettered age,
While,
    My healthy tum is greedy still
    Although it slopes a bit down hill.
    My rear spreads broadly o'er a chair
    And spends more time in resting there.

My eyes which once were set in white
Oft' now from pinkish pools give sight,
And,
    My hair which, latterly, was dark
    Now crowns my head with silver spark.
    My teeth are mostly with me still.
    That's thanks a lot to dentist's drill.

Life's streams have drained across my face
Eroding through a once-smooth race.
Now,
    Old frowns which sprung from furrowed rows
    Have cut twin creeks down to my nose,
    And smiles, I'm glad, not yet all wilted,
    Flow from my eyes in deltas, silted.

Fifty (*continued*)

> Maybe you ask: "How does he think
> Now that he's reached this old-age link?
> Err . . . ,
> > Does youth's wild pride support him still?
> > What has he learned for good or ill?"
> > And add: "Will we become like him,
> > As our minds grow to be as dim?"
>
> In truth, my views must seem quite tame
> Because so many turned out lame,
> So,
> > Of pride, I've now a smaller measure.
> > Instead, I've confidence to treasure,
> > And, of the two, I know which I
> > Would rather have as alibi.
>
> 'Mong things I've learned, of least appeal
> Was cruel Time's snail-slow reveal
> Of
> > My sad mistakes to blinkered me
> > While all around could plainly see.
> > My way to cope with this? Of course,
> > To temper you and smile on yours!
>
> Most lessons learned gave me alert
> Proportionate to how they hurt,
> But,
> > Of all things though, the best I've found
> > Is precious gold that's all around,
> > Not that aglow in jewell'ry fine
> > But there to dig from each heart's mine[1].

---

[1] *Acknowledgement: C J Dennis*

So, there I'll stop, perhaps part-way
Through what I'll maybe someday say.
It's
        My hope I'll get an old age long
        To sing with you Life's happy song
        Although, perhaps, too many a year
        And you could be too deaf to hear!

Australian Eucalypts

WILD puffs of wriggling, khaki leaves
    That jaunt above the loamy forest floor
Attend to ev'ry breath God daily breathes
And spark with lights imbibed through sky's broad door.
Responsive to caress of silent air
When sunshine bakes or evening stills the breeze,
They're frisky waves of fizzing, dancing flare
When winds stir up these charismatic trees.

No heed the toughness of their wood. Cries loud
For seas of roofs and roads and cattle plains
Will raze cathedral bush to chainsawn shroud
Abandoned by the wild of leaf-lined lanes.
Yet eucalypts, bred hard through fire and drought,
Still stand for beauty, strength and peace throughout.

Plants

INDUSTRIAL, multi-national, biochemical,
High-tech conglomerate, off-grid and solar powered,
Engaged in mass-producing foods and ethical
Green-sourced materials voraciously devoured
By tiered, pan-global clients in diverse income groups
Demanding service excellence, day in, day out
With ne'er a thought about the chlorophyllic hoops
That turn the wheels, or damage done by munching snout.

Each plant of jumbled, jitt'ring leaves is mannequin
For fashions of the day:- dew-flecked pyjamas worn
At dawn; white misty coats afloat in morning's thin,
Still air; smart bus'ness suits for when grey clouds adorn
The sky; and noontime's grinning greens that greet all eyes
At rest, above the mess of tasks and dreams our minds
Devise, to claim the em'rald jew'ls bright sun supplies.
All these displayed before cooled evening draws the blinds.

Animals

RECYCLERS, travellers, house keepers for the world,
Wild animals excel at any needed skill.
Exemplars, slaves and foods that propped great cultures furled,
Few dues are paid behind Mankind's self-pride and will.
The wheel was born from oxen, flight inspired by birds,
Civility and care were taught by many beasts,
Yet Man supplants these flowers with cursing words
And, sometimes, heartless rules imposed by blinkered priests.

Hard work and strength, sleek symmetry, soft grace and line
Were drawn from ants, lithe horses, snakes and darting fish
Before adoption as prized jewels in virtues's spine.
Such hard-won trophies welled from evolution's dish.
Admire the bugs enriching soils, the tardigrades
And velvet worms, like sponges in the sea, that cleaned
Through life's aeons. Sustainability parades
While we, from mines and landfilled wastes, are not yet weaned.

ANZAC rains

Rain is said to break a summer drought in Victoria on or around 25th April, the anniversary of the invasion of Gallipoli by Australian and New Zealand volunteers in the first world war.

THE RAINS that came at last
Awaited ANZAC Day
As if sad mem'ries past
Should pair with drought's dry play.
Instead of soldiers killed
And maimed by war's machine,
The countryside was grilled
In radiant, shimm'ring scene
That baked and hardened earth
As wartime hardens men
And sneered at living worth
Like battle's hellish den.

The rains that came at last
Have kissed the fields with green.
A stubble's growing fast
On Nature's cheek, still clean
From shaving, hungry jaws
Uprooting any stalk
They found on dusty floors.
And, if the plants could talk
Commotion would prevail –
A chance to put on weight,
To tint the umber vale
With blooms to celebrate!

The rains that came at last
Relieved the suff'ring trees
As armistice stopped blast
Of guns on killing sprees
In scenes distressed by stumps
Of woodlands blown to splints,

Fine homes collapsed to dumps
Of scrap round shells' death prints.
Maybe we folk could learn
The bush's stoic creed:
Though right and might may churn,
Fair living's all we need.

Fungus

Though fungus loosed for algal forebears rock-tied salts,
Allowing plants to move from sea to barren land –
Grand feat repaid by plants with tasty carbon vaults –
It now finds time to dine on morsels left to stand
Too long in stillest reaches of my kitchen's fridge.
A slice of bread, dalmation spots on, each green-tinged
And dew-drop whiskered, rests serene in privilege.
Elsewhere, a pot of fav'rite, creamy cheese unhinged
Is capped by mould as if to insulate from cold.
It's time to credit fungal scouts for being bold.

The fungal kingdom, oft forgot, has no less worth
To us than animals and plants we notice more.
Perhaps if fungus found a florist down-to-earth
Who liked to pick demure toadstools from musty floor
And pretty them in showy vase for shop window,
All folk would want to know, "Where do these gems come from?"
And, "What, I wonder, do they do at home but grow?"
Slick advertising's what they need, with much aplomb.

The Indecisivist

SOMETIMES I'm derided
For views undecided.
           The silly so-and-so's
           Want 'Yes's or 'No's
Not valuing a 'Hmmm'
Said with aplomb...mmm.
           I can easily choose
           To give or refuse
Deep deliberation,
Or long cogitation
           On asks of the day –
           Which ones though, I'm sorry,
                    I just can't say.

But, secretly, it's true,
Between me and you,
           Some things are too hard
           For this hard-working bard.
Oh! Whither shall I dither?
Whether hither or thither?
           Should I firmly vacillate?
           Promptly procrastinate?
Or refer to my load
And time off that I'm owed?
           You'll need to remind
           When work's piled up
                 and I'm getting behind.

Ginger Michaela

A reminder of the support women gave to the ANZAC soldiers in the first world war. All were volunteers.[2]

IT'S WAR! Please help! A far-off nation cries
And ev'ry svelte Australian buck begins
To search his slumb'ring soul, and agonise.
The choice: to stay at home as fam'ly prince
With comforts lush, maybe a girl to prize,
Or volunteer with risk to life and limbs,
Find courage, mateship, serve his manly role.
But, what for women, banned from gallant goal?

Australian women stayed behind to run
The farm, the shop, sustain the home and kids
While choking leaden fears for beau or son.
The blend of men and women, pans and lids,
So comforting in peace, had been undone.
Three hundred thousand men gone from their midst.
Few hist'ry books say how these women coped.
But some, to heed a call, with war eloped.

How mad! The generals thought a war was played
By men alone, without complaint, trained brave
To take their chance through deadly enfilade.
But soldiers, stretchered, needed care to save
Their lives, gain strength, re-whet ambition's blade,
The kindly care that women nurses gave
In makeshift wards, baked hot or frozen cold.
There, shattered men relearned what life might hold.

---

[2] Poem is adjusted from an entry to a competition run by the C.J. Dennis Society in 2016 with the theme of his touching, fictional, 'The Moods of Ginger Mick.' History and quotes of various Australian sisters (as represented by Michaela) selected from 'The Other ANZACS; Nurses at War 1914-1918' by Peter Rees (2008).

Ginger Michaela (*continued*)

Michaela sailed that year from Melbourne port.
She'd ice-blue eyes and wavy ginger curls,
Both tinder for the smiles of any Digger sort.
With scores of friends aboard for single girls,
Egypt arrived as if six weeks were short.
Then, trips to souk and sphinx, romance in whirls,
Wild, golden days and silver nights galore.
Mick sprang the bounds of country life before.

Calm came as troops embarked for Dardanelles,
The eerie calm . . . that hints of storm to come.
Michaela nursed at sea, in range of shells,
And logged her thoughts whenever; here are some :

> ". . 25thApril 1915: A most glorious Sunday . .
> . . the sound of distant heavy gunfire . .
> . . many wounded and dead from the beach . .
> . . dreadful wounds . . all were soaking wet . .
> . . badly wounded men . . crawling in from the
> barges . .
> . . We worked for 36 hours without stopping . .
> . . Shall never forget the awful . . hopelessness . .
> . . The flies swarmed . . the heat was
> suffocating . .
> . . Nothing will induce [us] to tell of the horrors
> we have seen . . "

Sometimes, Mick knew some patient there;
His death was then new pain to bear.

Galip'li lost, Michaela nursed the men
Shipped back to southern home as sick or maimed.
At Sydney, they were cheered, again, again;
Newspapers 'Our brave nurses' loud proclaimed.
'A bore', she thought, no plan of staying then,
Her call to save and serve, a voice untamed.
To Cairo where she found her life's romance
Before the willing ANZACs moved to France.

The brief war hoped was now no longer brief.
To Europe's guns and bombs was added gas
To blind and blister, Satan's leitmotif.
Michaela nursed them all in this morass
With scarcely food or sleep to bring relief.
But sharpest sting for this compass'nate lass:
Fiancé killed, discarded at Fromelles;
His last love note to follow in the mail.

When peace arrived at last, Michaela trod
Her wards as always, patients still in pain.
Respite was bliss, but grief remained to prod.
She lived, though never girl-at-heart again.
Less lucky, Nurse Cavell, at firing squad[3],
Said, "Patriotism is not enough", a plain
Command to tend the weak from either side.
Let strength in care re-form each nation's pride!

---

[3] Nurse Edith Cavell, executed 12 Oct 1915 for helping allied soldiers escape, even though she had often cared for enemy soldiers as well. See Wikipedia entry.

Bright Gleams the Dream

A villanelle. Use he/she.

Bright gleams the dream to make a child,
A child to love in any light.
So dark the path if she is wild!

Enchanting love held us beguiled.
Our eyes foretold the time was right.
Bright gleams the dream to make a child!

The babe enshrined, we reconciled
To jumbled day and sleepless night.
So dark the path if she is wild.

Convention mired her mind and riled.
Her will to be became our blight.
Bright gleams the dream to make a child?

The course of marriage sorely trialled
Grows harsh from barbs in caring's fight.
So dark the path if she is wild!

A childhood spent, a youth self-styled,
And we care-laden. "Will she write?"
Bright gleams the dream to make a child!
So dark the path if she is wild!

Land

REVERED in dreams by aborig'nal tribes,
Though mere commodity in others' thoughts,
Broad land, all rest and footfall circumscribes,
All fleeting deeds unfailingly supports.
The animals, un-kneeling, praise the land
Each day by study of its paths and drifts,
Respecting food and foes always at hand,
Alive to ebb and flow of seas'nal gifts.

But now, the owner takes the role of God,
Directing what will live and what will not.
The shading plants, and moisture-hugging sod
Are junk to any money-hungry clot.
The country from a thousand cuts slow dies,
Unsoothed by rains its sun-baked crust denies.

Sharks

WE DREAD the shark when swimming in warm sea,
Its lunge with pouting lips and razor teeth,
Our final breath as, wrenched from air to be
A fish's meal, we pass with just a wreath
Of trailing streaks of blood and bubbles – burped.
How mourners weep and hate the lissom shark
That hunts the sea for food, our role usurped
With never line, nor net, nor fishing barque.

How sharks revile the ocean tuna boat,
Its febrile pulse, shagreen of steel, pouting nets
Or razor hooks, the wrench from sea to bloat
On deck in air 'til, fins removed, Man lets
The tortured beast die slowly on sea bed.
This all for shark-fin soup and cats well fed.

Men!

I WISH I were a coat of fur
As warm as warm can be.
Then I could always wrap round her
Yet she would still feel free.

I wish I were a shower screen
A shield for missing gown.
Then I'd be sprinkled 'til she's clean
And next she'd rub me down.

I wish I were a brassiere
With cups as white as snow.
Then all day long I'd cradle her
And she would never know.

I wish I were a colt so free
With saddle firm and strong.
Then any day she'd ride on me
And never think it wrong.

Death

MURDER, gravest crime can be committed
Save when war bemedals those who slaughter:
Heroes, stoking memories unfitted
For convivial chat or merry laughter.
Yet, most life must kill to find a dinner
Tearing flesh and scrunching bones of weaker
Forms that do the same – or else get thinner.
Even plants trap flies in honeyed beaker.

Why need I distress at my impending
Death? Infinitesimal, atomic
Spot on Life's machine-belt singing, rending
Lives to food and dust routinely, tonic
For the soil and sea that roll forever.
Death, sharp spur for Life, all goals will sever.

A Macho Manager

I AM a modern manager.
    I've been to college too.
Politicos and share-holders
    consider me guru
And let me manage anything
    I understand or not
For which I pay myself howev-
    er much I think they've got.

They taught my craft with PowerPoint
    at managerial school.
We studied complex theories hard.
    It wasn't iv'ry tower.
But, looking back, I'll say of it
    there was one simple rule:
Expensive suit and massive car
    are all you need for power.

My hand-picked team of under-lead-
    ers works all day and night.
Their attitude is 'I can do'
    and surely 'Do it right'.
They listen well to every word
    I say or send email
But, if they think things by themselves,
    then they will surely fail.

How many people work for me,
    I really do not know.
I am a friend to none of them.
    It's bad for discipline.
Instead I send them circulars
    to show them they're below
With gen'rous use of gobble-d-gook
    to really rub it in.

A Macho Manager (*continued*)

When times are tough, reluctantly,
    I'm forced to cut down jobs
And hire consultant friends to help,
    and extra admin knobs.
The workers are so costly that
    I have to trim them down
Then take a bonus for myself
    lest under stress I drown.

I delegate 'most everything
    so I have time to think
Except of course important trips
    to places far away
Where I can learn what's going on
    and maybe rest or drink.
I keep the news just to myself
    'cos teaching doesn't pay.

I'm coming to retirement now.
    Thank heav'n for pension plan!
I've options too, quite rich it's true,
    all sheltered from taxman
And kindly paid from overheads
    and tax that's set aside.
One more is pert Ms Potts, Accounts,
    whose gifts are widely prized.

Inspiration

In loving memory of Mrs Fatme Mekawy, 'Tayta', my mother-in-law, married at 13, pregnant 16 times and mother to 10, died 25 May 2012, aged about 80.

Like a rock, flooded by the tide,
Tayta passed from us to Allah's right side.
Tears for her, salty like the sea,
Will oft refill our eyes where e'r we be.
Memories washing through the mind
Reveal no selfish deed of any kind.
Family fount of comfort and love,
She gave warmth to us all, like sunshine from above.
Her legacy, though poor, will never be spent:
Peace and kindness were her sole testament.
"When I die, be strong, don't weep.
I'll be content with my God, asleep."
And so, permanently, with no strong word,
She asserted her life and made herself heard.

Water is Everywhere – 7 Sketches

A PICTURE lies inverted on the silent lake
Until the bully, Wind, its morning breath has sighed
And smudged the paints to leave but mem'ries in its wake,
Replacing art with ruffled waves of anxious pride.
The wind's own art is for the animals that slake
Their thirst at water's edge. Damp vapours, air-born tide,
Alluring pictures for unmoistened noses make.

THE DARKENED pool that lies aside the river's course,
Seen still, yet slowly turned by sweep of waters by,
Invokes deep dreams from muddy, fish-concealing source,
Intriguing as the soul behind a horse's eye.
Unspoken thoughts, inspired by stare at wat'ry force,
Like floating leaves that drift within the current's tie,
Will surely, one day, Nature's peaceful rule endorse.

SALT, spumy waves that drive across an ocean's face
Reveal their beauty in cosmetic light of day
But, Jekyll-like, at night, pursue their evil race
Of rushing menace, stooped above the treach'rous way.
So disciplined as serried rows on water's space,
They're playful when they reach their goal at sandy bay,
And angry when assaulting cliffs in steadfast place.

Blue skies uplifting cotton clouds – like lily pads
Afloat on upside down lagoon – retain caprice
To brighten tourists seeing sights on outdoor gads,
Or, treat the dusty plains at last with drought's release.
Clouds, global flock of moody sheep, to windy fads
Beholden, are, one day, our bright protective fleece,
The next, a stormy gang of glow'ring, threat'ning lads.

Beneath the ground a senior reservoir awaits
Compressed between soil particles and massive rocks
That wall th'eternal dungeons of Hadean estates.
Free-flowing waters, once enliv'ning surface stocks,
Are downward dragged to stagnant pools in darkened straits,
And not released to light until the seaward locks
Are loosed, or farmer re-enslaves to pump that irrigates.

Earth's waters live as one amoeba sprawled from seas
To highest lands, its pseudopods in river beds
Sustained by rains condensing from the sky-borne breeze,
Slow eating food of loose-set sands from jutting heads.
This organism is cradle for all life at ease
If cared for, in return, by hallowed watersheds,
And spared the pois'nous wastes of careless Man's disease.

Life's waters lurk unseen in animated flesh
And seep through xylem tubes to highest leaves of plants.
Solutes and cells, undisciplined, uniquely mesh
To species whose infinite cast Earth's splendour grants.
Let not these hidden waters leak as tears shed fresh,
Or blood that flows where human ruthlessness implants,
Nor saps that ooze where business tramples Nature's creche.

The Oceans

COOL global bath, where continents recline
Massaged by tidal flows and slapping waves,
Where life arose from lightning, dust and brine
To thrive in climate that your mass enslaves,
You host, beneath your warmed and wind-blown streams,
Conveyors, icy cold yet fluid still,
Slow-sliding past abyssal, sun-starved dreams
Of eerie fish condemned to wait and kill.

You are a planet's planet, packed with life
And mysteries we hardly understand.
We merely gawp at hauled-up beauties rife,
Unmindful of sage ocean sense at hand.
What knowledge guides the turtle's lonely way?
What intellects inspire beneath the spray?

Air

AIR:- currency of life, distributed
To all untaxed, a communism veiled,
Connects green leaves to lungs, no thanks being said,
To raise and bind the myriad lives dovetailed.
Insouciant global trav'ller, moisture packed
In leaky swag drip-dripping rain and dew,
Transmits the motley news our ears enact
In concert hall for Earth's resounding crew.

Delight in cooling breeze on summer days
Or smarting cheeks from chast'ning slaps of frost.
Seek out the endless sweep of air's bouquets:-
Turned earth, a horse's sweat, young leaves fresh glossed.
Attend, eyes closed, pert Nature's sounds to hear . . .
Or watch the soaring birds held high on air.

Life Could be Verse

LOVE'S sweetness beckons young strong hearts
When hungry glances coincide
And eyes so thread their counterparts –
Like pearls on rays steadfastly tied –
That all freewill must shed its arts,
All happiness must be denied
Excepting that which frets and starts
As courting games, entwined, are tried.

    Love's practice captures free young lives.
    Soft handcuffs bind their willing souls
    As Nature's henchman so contrives
    To drag them from their former goals
    And press them with love's pass'nate drives
    Along the road that *he* controls
    Where worry's burden ever thrives
    And choice comes after fam'ly roles.

Love's magic glues two fertile seeds
Like well-cut dovetails for a drawer.
No earthly force but death succeeds
To disengage the bonded spore.
Three lives, as one, must answer needs –
Though courting's ardent course before
Ill trained each parent for their deeds,
Like cleaning mess from suff'ring floor.

    Love's nursery games enrich new minds
    That learn with hunger free from style.
    Experience, new skill unbinds,
    And listenings, new words compile.
    Thus patient parents open blinds,
    Revealing routes through life's long trial.
    Lament the child who never finds
    The paths that build a brain fertile!

Love's irksome calls will surely test.
The cries of selfish babies grate,
Impelling parents out of rest
From work and chores that dragged 'til late.
Who sees ahead these years so stressed?
Temptation sports its ugly bait:
More wealth or drink would calm me best!
Another love would ease my fate!

Love's challenges will test once more.
Young spirits swell as teen years run,
Imparting views that seem so sure.
All that is learned but never done
Ignites disdain for truths of yore
And thirsts new thoughts from anyone.
Now is the time to calm furore
By heeding young critiques unspun.

Love's river broadens out some day.
The waterfalls and rapids calm
As children find their shaky way
From where love sheltered them from harm.
And now, with luck, their lives repay –
With thoughtful deeds and youthful charm –
Parental years of home-bound stay.
All beasts that breed must crave such balm.

Love's sweetness binds two old weak hearts
When days streak by like hounds untied.
The years teach well the peaceful arts –
Obsessions past have cooled and died
While wrongs piled high in mem'ries' carts
Invoke the will to stand aside.
Togetherness their pathway charts;
Kind offspring summon love's new tide.

Underneath

OLD DEATH tip-toed right past my open door
When I was trudging on ambition's mill.
He smiled and said, "Why not stop work before
Your best years pass? Relax and live downhill."

    I looked at him and thought on this a while.
    "I love my work and people still need me,"
    I said but, underneath, I felt no smile.
    How long would I survive redundancy?

Another day, and Death was back to tease
While I was puffing on my jogging track.
"You're fat and look so strained and ill at ease,"
He said. "I'll wait for your first heart attack."

    "I'm working hard to get myself more fit,"
    I told, though fearing just what he had said.
    "*Your* cloak is full. You too could jog a bit."
    He leered: "I toll the heavy bell instead."

Next time Death called he was in frightful mood
And I bed-bound with cruel pain within.
He pressed his horrid face and ghastly hood
On window glass with chilling, smirking grin.

    "Be off," I said, "and stop your tricks with me."
    But, underneath, I knew he could be friend
    By granting ease and equanimity.
    For those, I could have taken hastened end.

Once more Death called, this time with stethoscope.
"You're weak and dying. I can do no more."
His face was sad but, underneath, was hope!
My anger was best medicine I knew:

    "Clear off!" I hissed with lips. (I couldn't shout.)
    "You can't have me . . . until the time is right
    . . . And I'll decide . . . that fateful day! Get out!"
    For, underneath, the flame still glowed, alight.

Vandalism in the Cemetery

MAKE no memorial for me,
Carved from unweathering stone,
Standing in hushed cemetery,
Badge of deathly time alone.
For, just one faded memory
Marking good deeds that I've sown
Would rest me more happily,
More at peace on my own.

So many dead folk on this earth
And too few stones to go round.
No stone can measure the worth
Of one idea that was sound,
Of one shared moment of mirth
Or one firm friendship found.
So, spare me the spiritual dearth
Of a gravestone on the ground.

Then, if old mem'ries should fade
As contemp'ries drift away
And all my deeds are out-played
By bold new heroes of the day,
I'll be no less repaid
Than those whose shiny granite lay,
No longer boasting flow'rs laid,
Resides forgotten in decay,
Long grass and cracks, vandal-made.

The Sea

ENCIRCLING shawl round Earth's appealing face,
Of shining turquoise silk, white flecked in lines
Across the wind that drives the rippling chase
Of waves 'tween sands and cliffs of lands' confines,
You hold your awesome strengths and deeps,
Your other-world of water-breathing lives
'Neath tantalising lucent roof that keeps
Your perfect sights and sounds in closed archives.

But is there now contest of power for Man
And Sea? Our catch, our warmth, our waste,
Like saboteurs, bring down your natural plan
For balanced, intricate food webs, tight laced,
That yield unending fish and wealth for folk
Who know enough, who stop before you're broke.

A Parliamentary politician

I AM a politician 'cause
        I think I know what's best.
I mostly talk at length so that
        all points are well addressed.
It would be nice to please you all
        so life could be more fun
But Lincoln said that kind of thing
        is rarely ever done.
So, when I speak in Parliament
        dressed up in formal suit,
It must be what the party thinks
        so I won't get the boot.
For me, that's not a problem though
        'cause my thoughts aren't rich fruit.

Sometimes I head out on the streets
        to meet the cheery folk
With ear to lend and time to spend
        on what they think is broke.
When passing a photographer
        I'll pause to shake a hand
And juggle smiles with frowns to seem
        a leader of the land.
Part of my job is to be seen
        in any public space
And place myself right at the front
        so all can see my face.
What use am I if no one knows
        I'm running in the race?

A Parliamentary politician *(continued)*

    Committees are my special'ty
        because my background's rich.
    I know a lot of useful things
        so members like my pitch.
    At times, though, others talk so much,
        it makes my buttocks ache –
    It's obvious their policies
        are just one big mistake.
    It's sad but true that many think
        most politicians poor.
    For sure, debates are rowdy to
        be heard across the floor;
    We mustn't let a member talk
        if known to be a bore.

    Unfortunately, new ideas
        are not things I can use.
    I have to sit upon a fence
        until the people choose.
    It's then I have a leading role
        to make the idea float
    Providing that it's cheap enough
        and won't upset my vote.
    Besides, electors like the old
        ideas recycled oft:
    More money here or there, tax breaks,
        and socialism's soft,
    And help the poor – I mix them all
        to get back in the loft.

    The pay and perks of Parliament
        aren't seriously bad
    But if you knew what I gave up
        you'd think that I was mad!
    At one time I was union boss
        and earned a pretty pack.

Then head-hunt made exec of me
        for even bigger whack.
Expenses are another thing
        that must be set quite high
I need a house at home and work
        and must between them fly,
And car, and office, PAs too,
        just so that I get by.

Thank heav'ns it's left to us to set
        how much we will receive
For stress of public life and laws
        from which there's no reprieve.
Our country needs the very best
        MPs that can be had,
A point that's lost by those who think
        that freedom's costs are bad.
No bribes should tempt us in the Parl-
        iament'ry talking house
When asked for help by needy friend
        who turns out as a louse.
I only help good patriots,
        directed to my spouse.

When all is said and done, we're drawn
        unblessed from human core
Just like the critic voting pub-
        lic that we're striving for.
We make the laws, and hire experts
        to write reports that rate
The evidence to keep our pol-
        icies bang up to date
– That's if we've time to understand
        and grasp the detailed text
And time to take the recs. well af-
        ter the election next.
Sharp turns along the straightest path
        would leave us all perplexed.

Wind

WATCH majestic trees respond-
    ing to a lively wind
And ask yourself if faithful monks
    could praise their honoured Gods
With more devotion. Knelt on earth,
    each tree, undisciplined,
Entranced by permeating power,
    shakes hard its wooden rods
In service to the breath of God
    with which all trees are twinned.

    Hear a powerful wind vibrate
        the harps strung tight in sheaves
    of twigs. Rough orchestra, untuned,
        on stage of earth and vines,
    Plays *presto* purr with canopy
        of loose-strung Aspen leaves,
    Or *piano* sighs with needle-furred
        she-oaks and bushy pines
    Until, *fortissimo*, weak play-
        ers fall and woodland grieves.

Oceans feel wind's storms unscathed,
    with laughing seabirds skewed
to skim the angry, toppling waves
    – virile sport to spice
Their lifelong window-shopping stare
    in search of plenitude.
But laughing seas' remorseless force
    as agent of wind's vice
Jousts callously with sailors' lives
    to win old rivals' feud.

Purpose has no role for wind.
    Existence only rides
The force that we may shelter from
    but never hope to tame.
To sense the holiness in it
    requires that our will bides
Unheeded for the time it takes
    our pestered souls to claim
The peaceful preaching that within
    a mod'rate breeze resides.

Coriolis' force directs
    wind's streams in playful curls.
No source can be identified,
    no destiny awaits.
Teamwork between the sun and air
    enforced aerobic swirls
Since Earth condensed from gas and will
    accept no other traits
While entropy is king of all
    but Nature's living pearls.

    Mix of moving molecules
        abrading one to one,
The wind is image of human-
    ity's mass ebb and flow.
Each one of us expressed from un-
    seen history respun,
Each one oft veering from an hon-
    est living's straightest throw
While moving anywhere on Earth
    until our breathing's done.

Separation

So you purchased a ride in the Devil's sports car,
Took a trip just for fun, leaving troubles afar,
Riding rainbows and clouds high aloft in the sky.
Grinning Devil he drove you, a helluva guy,
Telling jokes, looking round just to see that you laughed.
You felt free in the slipstream, hair raised by the draught,
Felt alive in the colours that wafted around,
Free of burdens you left near your road on the ground,
The long road you need walk for your life to be found.

    Do you think of tomorrow, the ways you could take?
    Will there always be help when your Devil hits brake
    And you've stepped from the car, sitting down by the road
    Looking back where you've come, felt the old heavy load
    You must bear on the journey uphill all the time,
    Shy of folk who could ease the long ache of your climb?
    There's a road past the cliffs of depression and thrills,
    A road calling for talents you've got and your skills –
    The long road you need walk before energy stills.

We see darkness descend when you've stepped from that car.
Your head's drained of all joy when you're back where we are.
"Let my house be burned down", you once said without care,
"With me in it", you added, a cry of despair.
Then the doctor and dentist and chemist were bad,
A past lover was coming to break all that you had,
Even Mum talked about you, disrupted your life,
Things I know to be false because she's my wife.
You'll not stay the long road in a mood of such strife.

Please remember our training for bringing you up
Gave us only one chance to help you drink the cup.
Leave the Devil alone, find a plainer life style.
Give it time and your strength, help others awhile
To help you to be free. You'll make friends on that road,
Perhaps someone who bears a yet heavier load.
Subtle pleasures are there on the road that is real
And they last, unlike dreams from fast automobile.
Just the walking that road is a comfort to feel.

Postscript:
And from where did it come, that sports car that you took?
Was it kids in your class who drove you off the hook?
Or the man looking after the skateboarding park
Who abused green teenagers intent on a lark?
Then you filled in a form for a prof who prescribed
Strongest drugs of dependence that may be imbibed.
He said he could help you but you were taken away
Psychotic, deluded, and abject one day.
Now a psych sends amphetamines, given you pay.

My Faithless Religion

MY SACRED temple, roofed by gall'ried sky
On columns firm, the taut, supportive trees,
Is walled by hills and mountains standing by
And hums with plainsong chants, soft-mouthed by breeze.
Mosaic patterns decorate the floor
With zig-zag-sided, dapple coloured tiles.
Dividing channels shimm'ring waters pour,
Sustaining life in endless, perfect styles.
Green tapestries adorn the ample rooms
Festooned with floral sequins, tinted fair,
Haphazard weave of Nature's tousled looms,
Perfused with incense strong: the plain fresh air.

> I meditate while sky-born songs entrance
> And flick'ring leaves add rustling, silky drone.
> Whose God, I dream, assembled these from chance?
> Whose God conceived such beauty on Her own?
> Tonight, this architect'ral masterpiece,
> First, flooded by the sunset's amber light,
> Is darkened, diff'rent magic to release:
> High glimpse of sparkling, calming infinite.
> Eternal life is all around to see,
> Evolving power, seeded not designed.
> What blindfold games grew from my piety,
> My faith installed by birth, my strutting mind!

But beauty, lacking care, can never save
From grinding chores, harsh pain or trembling fear.
Sweet life and love are golden things we crave
Amidst the work and suff'rings hard to bear.
Yet, salmon swim a thousand hostile leagues,
The penguin cares through lashing polar night,
Shy beasts all fear toothed raptor's cold intrigues –
A life of ease is fortune, not a right.
Like nested fledglings squabbling to survive,
Rough contests were the gates that let us through.
Today we know respect as prize to drive,
Ennobling humble folk, good losers too.

    Our human woes from humans mostly come.
    Each yearns for glitt'ring place before the crowd –
    None more than fiends who hear Faith's snaring drum
    As cue to ravage lives and cultures proud.
    My saints, though strong to pierce the crowd, are shy
    With simple speech, plain-faced, arousing none.
    Unsermoning, they show sound paths to ply
    While life is green and dying unbegun.
    Commandments have I none, nor critic priest.
    My deeds are weighed on balanced scales
    Against the rules agreed from west to east.
    The swinging pointer cuts when honour fails.

No prayers do I murmur on my road.
I praise my modest God by stepping out,
Exploring, sharing gifts on me bestowed
Like petals blown – for me to turn about.
My holy book distills all those before,
Recounting good and bad in ev'ry race,
Forever honing Time-assented law,
The law that sparks in any human face.
My Heaven is here and now, if not oppressed.
My rest needs toil, my joy needs stress; it is
With balance that my days are fully blessed,
My worthy goals achieved, my lifetime's riches.

    Evangelists clutch tight my arm and say:
    "Believe our holy book and God will save."
    A thousand faiths! A million deaths today!
    Whose faith is truth? Whose soul will jump the grave?
    I have no sanctity to shelter me
    From foreign ways or customs I eschew,
    Nor sacred verses crammed in memory,
    Tight strangling brave new thoughts arising through.
    So many faiths divide and leave us torn;
    Their programmed priests can only disagree.
    I seek the laws of God 'mong reason's corn
    Top-sown on common lands of honesty.

My Faithless Religion (*continued*)

No shame or praise will ever fire my corpse:
Before my birth I knew the endless void!
The lives of others spin the textured warps
That earthly days permit to be enjoyed.
Each day with light is holiness for me,
The folded rocks of God's titanic whim,
And crumbling fossils of antiquity,
True relics from the path we took from Him.
Some things I will aver: that life is brief –
To fill it well is thus my pleasant goal;
Five senses, true or tricked, build my belief;
And kindness, giv'n or savoured, floats my soul.

OUR universe that clasps the formless sky
In galaxies spread to eternity,
Where Time itself is summer butterfly
That spawned the train of Life's diversity
On gen'rous Earth beneath the Sun's warm eye,
Providing all we need, that makes us free:-
This universe, for me, can qualify
As God, as ever-present Deity.
This human dream is all I need to try
To give unpaid as God has giv'n to me,
To hope for courage ready when I die,
And live meanwhile as I'd have others be.

Freedom

Take pleasure from kind freedom's gifts:-
A stroll at dusk, the time to dream
Along whichever path uplifts,
The chance to buy the kids ice cream,
Select the food upon your plate,
Or share with folk who care to hear
Your thoughtful words in fair debate.
Put on the clothes you like to wear
And, if distinct you want to be,
Don't shrink at all from oddball ways –
Your boldness can help others free
Resented ties of social stays.

These gifts you may recall when life
Grips firmer, even cruelly tight,
When money's gone, disease is rife,
Or, pressed so hard, no thoughts come right.
Who can expect to skirt these rocks,
If ever living years unstressed?
Don't wait for Fate's unwelcome knocks
Before you find the simplest best.

Index of first lines

A bold man who's intent on romance . . .	2
Air:- currency of life, distributed . . .	27
A picture lies inverted on the silent lake . . .	24
Beneath the ground a senior reservoir awaits . . .	25
Blue skies uplifting cotton clouds – like lily pads . . .	25
Bright gleams the dream to make a child . . .	16
Cool global bath, where continents recline . . .	26
Dear vultures all, you've gathered here . . .	5
Earth's waters live as one amoeba, sprawled from seas . . .	25
Encircling shawl round Earth's appealing face . . .	32
Endless, clasping mesh of whispy, fungal . . .	3
Gentle reader, perhaps you've some time for a rhyme . . .	vi
I am a modern manager . . .	21
I am a politician 'cause . . .	33
I love the leaves . . .	4
Industrial, multi-national, biochemical . . .	8
It's war! Please help! A far-off nation cries . . .	13
I wish I were a coat of fur . . .	19
Life's waters lurk unseen in animated flesh . . .	25
Like a rock, flooded by the tide . . .	23
Love's sweetness beckons young strong hearts . . .	28
Old Death tip-toed right past my open door . . .	30
Our universe that clasps the formless sky . . .	42
Make no memorial for me . . .	31
Murder, gravest crime can be committed . . .	20
My sacred temple, roofed by gall'ried sky . . .	40
Recyclers, travellers, house keepers for the world . . .	9
Revered in dreams by aborig'nal tribes . . .	17
Salt, spumy waves that drive across an ocean's face . . .	24
Sometimes I'm derided . . .	12
So you purchased a ride in the Devil's sports car . . .	38
Take pleasure from kind freedom's gifts . . .	43
The darkened pool that lies aside the river's course . . .	24
The rains that came at last . . .	10
Though fungus helped old seaweed forebears find the salts. . .	11

Watch majestic trees responding to a lively wind . . .	36
We dread the shark when swimming in warm sea . . .	18
Wild puffs of wriggling, khaki leaves . . .	7
Your day's work starts with glowing, velvet hold . . .	1

www.ingramcontent.com/pod-product-compliance
Lightning Source LLC
Chambersburg PA
CBHW020331010526
44107CB00054B/2069